ALBERTO PINTO
Orientalism

ALBERTO PINTO

Orientalism

RIZZOLI
NEW YORK

Published in the United States of America in 2004
by Rizzoli International Publications, Inc.
300 Park Avenue South
New York, NY 10010
www.rizzoliusa.com

Original edition copyright © Éditions Flammarion, Paris, 2004
English edition copyright © 2004 Rizzoli International Publications, Inc.

Layout: Alain Pouyer
Translation: William Wheeler

Printed at Canale, Italy

ISBN: 0-8478-2672-4

FRONT COVER: View of a Moroccan patio.
BACK COVER: In Egypt, an intense Delacroix-red drawing room embodies the essence of literary Orientalism.
PRECEDING PAGE: Interior patio of a residence opening onto a red drawing room.

Table of Contents

We would like to thank all the persons who assisted
in the realization of this project:
Danièle Turquais Cerdan, Yves Pickardt, Nicolas Dufour,
and especially Amr Mandour.

Our thanks also go to the staff of Alberto Pinto's Studio
for their warm welcome and judicious advice.

Alberto Pinto has remained true to his Mediterranean origins. It is apparent in his love of luxuriant gardens and of associating precious materials and playing with natural light. Actually, he adheres to an interpretation of the Oriental spirit with its constant appeal for the Western eye while never forgetting the need for comfort. Whether they be for palaces in North Africa, or Syrian bedrooms and Oriental patios imagined for European homes, his interior designs

are all invitations for the reader to set out on a long journey in search of the colors of the Orient from Marrakech to Tangiers, via Lisbon and Paris. We thus follow in Alberto Pinto's footsteps during his aesthetic itineraries in an admittedly expected decorative register but one in which he demonstates exactness, culture and especially modernity. Orientalism, however, is not for him a decorative failsafe steeped in effortless nostalgia. He knows how to orchestrate this specific art while unveiling its charged past, nomadic influences and more especially, he knows how to update it.

He often reinvents Orientalism avoiding excessive caricatures while adapting Moroccan or Egyptian, Syrian or Ottoman art to modern interiors. And as the eye of the decorator loves to juggle with unusual aesthetics, he ingenuously contrives dialogues between different or contrasting cultures in his projects. Without a doubt this is a constant in Alberto Pinto's work: combining to the point of astonishment Oriental cultures like so many voyages around the Mediterranean basin which come to an end in the Far East. His vision of the Orient is a very personal one which permits him to hang European paintings in Moorish alcoves or to add Indian touches to arabized decors.

The key to Orientalism according to Alberto Pinto is observation. For example, the gaze of Western culture which once it has discovered the Orient and has fallen under its fascination, sets about to

In the green and white drawing room of a Moroccan residence, a ceramic parrot under stucco stalactites.

interpret it, to play with transcultural aesthetics. Consequently, Orientalism is always an interpretation, a mixture of cultural expressions and in his interiors more than elsewhere.

Often Alberto Pinto's interiors cultivate a very literary Orientalism like that practised by the French naval officer and author Pierre Loti which teemed with innumerable references and subtle dissynchronizations. Pointed Ottoman arches open onto a Chinese drawing room while a Persan bedroom is adjacent to a pale green Moroccan bathroom. A sedate blue and white bedroom of Berber inspiration contrasts with the deep red luster of a drawing room evoking Delacroix, the sunshine filtering through the moucharaby and reverberating off the traditional tiling. Mirrors reflect to infinity precious woods and mother-of-pearl marquetry; the carved white stucco draws its inspiration from Eastern calligraphy.

This book is an Open, Seseame to interiors that have no port of call but constitute unique realms at once filled with familiar yet strikingly novel memories.

In the foyer of a Moroccan residence, the portrait of a Maharajah after Winterhalter and an antique Syrian copper chandelier with gold and silver inlays.

Around a courtyard in Morocco

Oriental homes often present austere, closed exteriors whereas the warm,
exuberantly decorated interiors open onto luminous, interior courtyards.

After Alberto Pinto was commissioned to outfit this Oriental residence, he articulated his design around an interior patio decorated using traditional models of *gebs,* highly wrought carved plaster. The abundant decoration in this stylistic exercise transforms the white space into a small lexicon of decorative ornamentation.

Guests arrive in the interior courtyard through a small, white, sunlit vestibule with high windows fitted with moucharaby screens. Accentuated by the immaculate whiteness of the walls, the luminosity is startling. This is an elegantly ambivalent space, a liminal space beyond the exterior but not yet the interior. The open architecture and the white arcades obviously bring to mind the grand courtyards of Oriental palaces. Nonetheless, the refined, strict lines of the seat furniture and the glimpses of the rooms off the patio divulge the voluptuous comfort of Moroccan interiors.

A large Mogul copper brazier draws the eye to the center of the courtyard. Enveloped by the high ceilings of the gallery surrounding it, the patio is a veritable architectural exercise. This is the nucleus of the residence: all the rooms and activities—private and reception spaces, drawing rooms, dining area, and offices —converge here. There is also an access to the garden through a wooden door off the patio.

OPPOSITE: Calligraphic designs in gebs run vertically on the arcades flanking the perspective. An oversized copper lantern stands guard.
PRECEDING PAGE: In the vestibule of the residence, high narrow windows line the waxed plaster walls. Turned wooden moucharaby screens let the sun enter to light an antique Egyptian chandelier.

Moroccan artistic expertise includes gebs, the traditional craft that produces lace-like surfaces from carved and shaped plasterwork, but also copperwork and woodworking. Hanging from the gallery ceilings and walls, the Egyptian lanterns vie for attention with their openwork arabesques and Arabic calligraphy as they filter the subdued evening light, turning the white decor a warm amber. Syrian mother-of-pearl inlaid wood settees lining the gallery walls directly echo the openwork panels and moucharabies.

OPPOSITE: Three Egyptian copper lanterns with silver inlays festoon the gallery ceiling.
ABOVE: Syrian settees flank the monumental wood door.
PRECEDING PAGES: The rigorous organization of the square patio is magnified by the profusion of decorative plasterwork.
FOLLOWING PAGES: From the center of the courtyard, guests can catch a glimpse of the privates suites protected behind high, solid cedar doors.

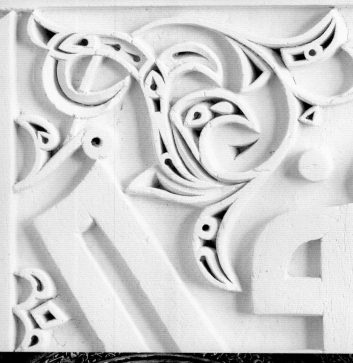

In this restained and whimsical, ardent and strict space, architecture and decoration are on equal footing. The architecture is assertive and the decoration adds lightness and grace to the symmetrical composition of repeating large semicircular arches and the smaller horseshoe-shaped ones and the massive pillars in the four corners of the courtyard. Opening onto all of the rooms, small decorative windows called *chemmassiats* in Arabic punctuate the gallery, while delicate *geb* festoons run along the tops of the arches and temper their bulkiness.

The plant-inspired arabesques of the *tawriq* motifs develop deep within the thickness of the walls, setting in play a game of light and reflections. Like ephemeral inscriptions traced in pristine sand, Kufic calligraphy frames the arches and underscores the panels. Knotwork, palmettes, spikes, and kernels are standard elements in Tachjir decoration, where the tree often provides inspiration for ornamentation. They form the verses of a poem unfurling as it turns around the courtyard walls. Like a reflection of the inlaid floor, the network of wooden struts and braces supporting the glass roof breaks up the sunlight. Contrasting with the luminous white walls, the openwork of the dark cedar beams and coffering in the Egyptian tradition adds a masculine feeling unlike the delicate arabesques of the *gebs*. The decorator has orchestrated a balance between rigor and exuberance.

RIGHT: Hanging over the central Mogul brazier, a copper openwork lantern designed by Alberto Pinto and crafted in Morocco reflects the light it receives through the glass roof.

OPPOSITE FROM TOP TO BOTTOM: Detail of the plaster knotwork of a chemmassiat; *detail of a calligraphic frieze; decorated with the same ornamental vocabulary of interlacings and calligraphy, metal adds warmth to the dominant white.*

FOLLOWING PAGES: Opening onto the patio, a Syrian desk inlaid with mother of pearl echoes the decorative elements of the courtyard.

Between the patio and the office, grand cloisonné doors reveal a horseshoe-shaped opening. Here space is of reduced proportions and the decoration particularly refined. The office basks in generous light penetrating through highly wrought iron grilles that protect windows of Spanish influence.

In the strong zenithal sun, the grilles almost disappear in the backlight. Ricocheting off the inlaid mother-of-pearl segments covering the furniture, light actually becomes a first-class decorating material.

The Orientalist treatment combining images of the Levant and the West is appropriately expressed in the furniture design. Recalling the patio settees, the characteristic Syrian craftsmanship of mother-of-pearl inlays on walnut here has undergone a stylistic Westernization. The legs on the desk and the armchairs have a Louis XV curve while the excessive volutes on the chair backs are decidedly Oriental.

OPPOSITE: *Detail of the Syrian desk.*
LEFT FROM TOP TO BOTTOM: *The unexpected juxtaposition of an Oriental frieze and simple stripes adds a contemporary ambience; opposites attract as the matte of Egyptian albaster presents the perfect foil for the iridized mother of pearl; the updated color scale chosen by Pinto was directly inspired by those of Oriental fabrics.*

A Moroccan majlis

*Oriental hospitality finds its most refined expression in
the vast drawing rooms lined with deep divans piled
with plush cushions. Like the divan, Moroccan* majlis *are almost
obligatory stylistic exercises.*

Engraved copper, buff enamel, ocher, and polished wood: in this drawing room the chromatic scale is a warm *camaieu*. In keeping with the mood, animal-skin velvets cover the cushions. This is not without a certain irony, recalling the big game hunts during the Raj, while India was under British rule. Alberto Pinto sets in motion here a game he loves and plays masterfully, as one "Orient" is exchanged for another. These are concepts and images seen and transformed through Western eyes; memories of mythical and aesthetic voyages to lands so, so far away, where the history of the Middle East and the geography of India and China blur in the minds and the tastes of Western aesthetes.

OPPOSITE AND RIGHT: Antique Iberian and Moroccan ceramics are grouped on the end tables and the central coffee tables. The warm tints of the motifs respond to those of the tiger and leopard velvets and the wood.
FOLLOWING PAGES: On the right wall, a large painting depicting three Arab women in traditional dress seated in a garden encapsulates Western fantasies about the Orient.
PRECEDING PAGE: A pair of antique Syrian wooden mirrors with ivory and mother-of-pearl inlays adds depth to the room whose narrow dimensions facilitate conversation.

While the Syrian office played on the differences that opposed it to the adjoining patio, this private drawing room emulates its luminosity and style. It takes up the same geometric interlacings in a simpler version; here they are stenciled and painted on the walls in soft, light tints of pale yellow, off-white, and a light earth color.

On the sill of the small decorative *chemmasiat* window, a grouping of antique *objets d'art* form a very painterly still life.

On the patio the calligraphic inscriptions are one with *gebs* plasterwork whereas here it is more a pretext. Walls are lined with a collection of framed calligraphic pages and fragments. Engraved in wood, embroidered in silk, and drawn in ink, the suras from the Koran, proverbs, and poetry are treated as full-fledged works of art.

ABOVE: View of a corner of the divan, brightened by sunlight coming off the courtyard.
LEFT: A reflection of the calligraphy collection in a mother-of-pearl inlaid mirror.

Designed by Alberto Pinto, the coffered ceiling of the *majlis* is a masterpiece of Egyptian artisanship. He has intermingled various woods, bone, and metal in numerous motifs that bring into play a complete repertoire of forms. The arabesque bands of the *chemmasiat* windows, geometric motifs, the plant-inspired interlacing, and other tawriq designs all communicate without repetition. By varying forms, materials, color intensity, and scale of the panels, the coffered ceiling is a brilliant style exercise.

ABOVE AND RIGHT: The coffered cedar ceiling carved and inlaid with bone, copper, and rare wood veneers is an exceptional example of traditional craftsmanship.

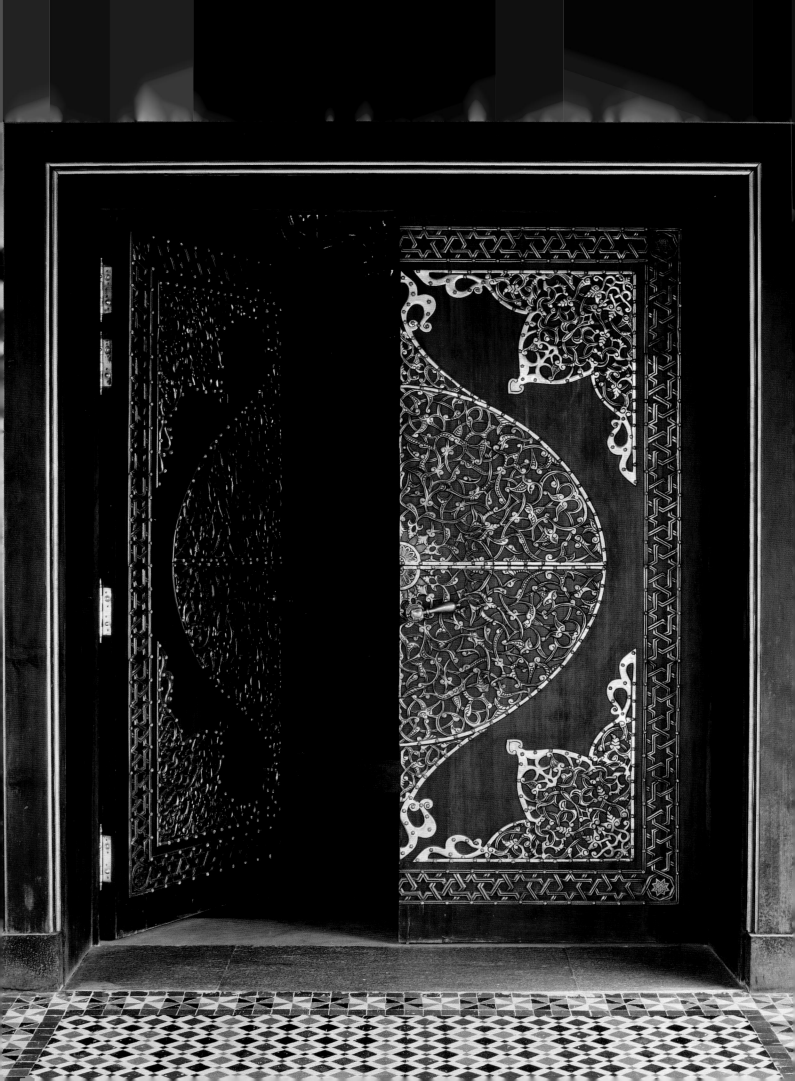

Receptions in
a summer house

Traditionally in great houses in the Orient a reception area is reserved
for guests, where all signs of intimacy are restrained and the force of protocol
is sensed room after room.

Behind the main bronze-inlaid walnut door in the Oriental tradition opens a large Hispano-Moorish vestibule with a brown, green, and pearly dado. Deep green-enameled Portuguese bowls hanging on the walls echo the tints of the Moroccan ceramics. The imposing Portuguese table and the Syrian armchairs set a stately ambience in the majestic antechamber. The walls are a series of arcades in traditional plasterwork, featuring the characteristic plaster stalactites widely used in Hispano-Moorish architecture. An extraordinary flower garden unfolds behind these inner walls and the sliding moucharaby screens. Round tables and matching Syrian marquetry chairs stand under large amber-colored Murano glass chandeliers. They illuminate the painted panels covering the ceiling.

PAGE 42: The bronze main doors.
PAGES 44 TO 47: Two views of the Hispano-Moorish vestibule.
PAGE 48-49: The reception dining room.
LEFT: Detail of the marquetry furniture and the embroidered upholstery.
OPPOSITE: Details of the mother-of-pearl marquetry and the traditional Moroccan tiling.

The reception rooms are richly ornate in a warm chromatic scale of reds and golds. The Turkish rug, the ceramic tiles, and the paneling evoking stamped Cordovan leather; all play on a deep red theme. Guests pass through carved wooden doors covered with sophisticated strapwork and brightly painted illuminated designs—a perfect example of Moroccan painted decoration—on their way to the rooms beyond.

ABOVE AND OPPOSITE: The doors leading to the reception rooms, closed and open.
FOLLOWING PAGES: The Murano chandelier and the painted ceiling in the dining room.

Alberto Pinto took his inspiration for the guest vestibule from Mamluk designs found in Egyptian residences. Although they served as the direct point of departure for this space, these designs were freely interpreted on the walnut and mother-of-pearl marquetry furniture executed by Egyptian craftsmen.

OPPOSITE: Armchairs and low tables standing on a Moroccan rug woven in the Middle Atlas face a majestic cabinet fitted with sinks. Above, the cornice of the mirror was inspired by a Mamluk design.
ABOVE: Three identical mother-of-pearl marquetry doors.

Oriental tables
in Tangiers

In the East the nomad instinct is widely accepted.
In his home in Tangiers, an aesthete takes great fun in surprising guests
with dressing tables in the most unexpected places.

On the patio two small private drawing rooms have been arranged in alcoves, the walls covered with warm traditional painted patterns softly lit by an antique oil lamp. The master of the house enjoys setting tables in yellows and golds against the black of night. The saffron and coral tablecloth and napkins pick up the bold tones of the plates designed by Alberto Pinto with Ottoman characters. These are the dominant colors stated throughout the room, from the embroidered cushions on the divan to the repoussé copper chandelier, the red Moroccan rug, and in even more muted tones, the Anglo-Indian armchairs in woven straw. The transparency of crystal reflects in the silver on the table.

OPPOSITE FROM TOP TO BOTTOM: Traditional white embroidery on a saffron background on the sofa; an antique Turkish silk cushion on the armchair; the Ottoman porcelain designed by Alberto Pinto.
RIGHT: Under a copper chandelier, Anglo-Indian woven straw seating surrounds the table for an intimate dinner.
PRECEDING PAGES: On the alcove walls hang The Moorish Café *by Gustave Lino and* The Prayer *by Nicola Forcella.*

Private dinners are often organized in the library off the patio. Guests enter the striped-covered room through a 19th century embroidered Turkish door curtain decorated with pink and bordeaux calligraphic designs. The color scheme is echoed on the table covered with an embroidered throw and set with ceramic plates with figures inspired by Persian miniatures. Anglo-Indian furniture lends nostalgic exoticism. Rinceaux and Arabic floral patterns flow around the door curtain and down to the table, enveloping the guests in a gourmet fantasy.

PRECEDING PAGES: View of the library through the 19th century Turkish door curtain.
OPPOSITE FROM TOP TO BOTTOM: Details of embroidery on the Persian tablecloth and the gold and silk door curtain.
RIGHT: On the table the designs on the ceramic plates were inspired by Persian miniatures.

In the middle of the Oriental-style drawing room, a silvery dinner table has been prepared on a low table close to the red striped velvet divan. The silk embroidered tablecloth with inlaid mirrors is from India, and the mother-of-pearl plates and the silver are Turkish, Mogul, and European; everything captures and throws back shimmering reflections in the subdued lighting. Behind, the divans are lined with embroidered wedding cushions from Fez, which contrast with the walls covered with painted geometric designs in shades of beige.

PRECEDING PAGES: *Against the backdrop of a quiet conversation corner with a divan, and under a 19th-century painting by Gyula Torah depicting an Oriental dancer, a dinner table has been improvised.*
LEFT: *A Mogul ewer with a bird beak is surrounded by silver vases and bouquets of yellow roses.*
OPPOSITE FROM TOP TO BOTTOM: *Red velvet, an Agra rug from India, and Fez embroideries play tone on tone.*
FOLLOWING PAGES: *Turkish cups, Tiffany Orientalist coffeepots, and 19th-century Italian crystal stand on matching Turkish tables.*

From his travels to the legendary cities of the East, the master of the house has brought back marquetry gueridons, which comprise a magnificent collection. Ottoman, Syrian, or Egyptian, each tells the story of a country, its artisans, and craft techniques. Most are in walnut inlaid with mother of pearl, bone, tortoiseshell, or ebony. Some also are decorated with silver filigree or with specific motifs like the calligraphic inscription of the name of the craftsman or the patron in the center of one of the gueridons.

OPPOSITE: Three examples of walnut and mother-of-pearl marquetry: star patterns, an ebony cabochon, and a calligraphic inscription with a flower. RIGHT AND PRECEDING PAGES: The collection of gueridons displayed on a Moroccan rug.

A literary drawing room

Often the Orientalist style is symbolized by the French author Pierre Loti,
whose cultivated taste for the accumulation of Arabic souvenirs
remains an unsurpassed reference.
This interior is a perfect example of this style.

The drawing room is an intense Delacroix red, and with its Venetian glass chandeliers, snips and touches of Chinese and Thai in the furniture, the harem scenes in the paintings, and Persian rugs, the room embodies the essence of literary Orientalism: teeming with allusions, a melancholic, adventurous spirit, and unexpected associations.

The Orient here is restored and repurposed. The paintings all narrate idealized stories of sensual Arabian beauties, languishing under palace arches, adorned with jewels, recumbent on divans in the privacy of alcoves.

More overly exotic effects complete this Western phantasm. For instance, ideas for some furnishings have been retrieved from long, nostalgic voyages. In the alcove two Chinese lacquered commodes face off, surmounted by large, matching Thai mirrors, whose exuberant design spills over into the intimate corner organized around the fireplace. A collection of tall, copper repoussé ewers continue the ambient eclecticism.

This romantic approach to the Orient is quintessentially theatrical. Decked in reds, the staging of this Verdi-esque tragedy is the perfect decor for divas. the stylistic allusion is definitely Napoleon III, which works well with warm colors and nocturnal lighting. Designed like a jewel presentation case, the interior is red from top to bottom. The ceiling is covered with painted wood decoration with medieval, Persian, and Ottoman references. Geometric designs, *rinceaux,* and arabesques clad the walls, revealing inspiration from the Alhambra, illuminated manuscripts, and Middle Eastern temples. The interior weds twisted Western bands and traditional Hispano-Moorish corbels. The end product is without distinct provenance, an elegant nowhere from here and there and still elsewhere.

PRECEDING PAGES: A corner of the Napoleon III drawing room.
LEFT: The ceiling is a compendium of decorative styles.
RIGHT: Details of two antique wedding sashes and traditional embroidery, all Moroccan.
FOLLOWING PAGES: The Bohemian chandelier against the painted ceiling.

Suite in a date grove

Orientalism as championed by Alberto Pinto is not limited to
nostalgic reconstitution.
He also creates this rich atmosphere in contemporary spaces, as in this suite.

Between cedar columns surmounted by imposing carved mahogany capitals and under languorous, abandoned women on canvas, a vast bed is the focal point of this octagonal bedroom, which seems to be prepared for a visit from Sardanapal, the legendary tyrant immortalized by Eugène Delacroix. Double marquetry doors open to a modernized Orientalism, and unencumbered comfort is the keyword. The soft Moroccan rug designed by Alberto Pinto responds to warm ocher walls and the antique *susanis* on the bedcover and cushions. Surrounding the bed, the gold-framed paintings of female figures are part of classic Orientalist imagery. A suite of furniture in a 1940s spirit, a Murano glass lamp, and a Syrian mother-of-pearl inlaid table have been arranged under a delicate but imposing Egyptian lantern. Designed by Alberto Pinto, the headboard and the night tables were inspired by a 1930s design and recreated in mother-of-pearl, ebony, and lemonwood marquetry.

The bathroom is in earth colors, ochers, and black. A collection of Egyptian alabaster *objets d'art* have been grouped on matching shelving units. The dressing room is accessible through the large doors with carved openwork, outfitted with mirrors behind. Although this is a highly practical zone, once the doors are closed, the mystery of the Indian inspiration takes over, and the hallway leads to an Oriental neverneverland.

PRECEDING PAGES: *Above a Syrian table,* The Gifts *by Henry-Leonce Darrica hangs across from an armoire and a 19th-century Syrian mirror.*
RIGHT: *Details of two wedding sashes and a Moroccan door hanging.*
FOLLOWING PAGES: *Adjacent to the bedroom, the bathroom and dressing room both represent an audacious design melting pot, bringing together the Middle East and India.*

When a guest enters the sauna, he loses all reference to time. This feeling is intensified by a total lack of natural light. The wall mosaics are equally instrumental in creating this time warp, as they bring to mind archaeological digs in North Africa as well as early 20th-century bathhouses. The cold-water pool, the silver-plated bucket and ladle, and the marble floor are pure Oriental, and the Art Deco floral mosaic designs covering the pillars are thus all the more disorienting.

LEFT: The Art Deco floral mosaics display the exceptional craftsmanship of Moroccan artisans.
OPPOSITE: View of the sauna.

At once alcove, boudoir, and vestibule, this room marks the passage toward the private suites with muted lighting. The sun arrives solely through an elegant loophole window, and color takes over the role of lighting. In order to enhance the intimate atmosphere, the dark wood of the paneling, the door, and the carved ceiling as well as the haute époque Portuguese table interact with the rest of the Oriental furniture in the room. Highly contrasting oranges and greens cover the divan nestled in the alcove and also the seats of the Egyptian armchairs. Behind the divan the wall panels are decorated with orange and blue plant-inspired arabesques, which, because of their symmetry, are viewed as through an abstract veil. The fabrics covering the divan and the cushions are hand-embroidered in the Moroccan tradition with age-old star and geometric patterns. They are proof of the good health of local artisanship.

LEFT: *Entirely decorated with highly colored ornamentation, the alcove is surmounted by a carved wood lintel with intricate scrolling in the Turkish style.*
OPPOSITE: *Details of the divan embroidery and the painted decoration of the alcove.*
FOLLOWING PAGES: *In the boudoir, 19th-century Persian wedding contracts hang on the wall above ivory and tortoiseshell coffers presented on a turned-wood table.*

Conceived as an inner sanctum, the office is completely lined with painted paneling directly inspired by Moroccan Berber designs. However, the colors chosen by the master of the house, a deep blue contrasting with a vivid yellow, are a departure from tradition. The white sofa and a pastel by Henry d'Estienne of a young Arabic bride appear as luminous touches in an otherwise masculine atmosphere. The bone-inlaid ebony desk and the walnut armchairs with moucharaby panels are from 19th-century Egypt.

PRECEDING PAGES: *The office walls adjacent to the boudoir are decorated with wood friezes in the same dark blue and golden yellow as the remarkable carved and painted door.*
LEFT: *A group of Egyptian furniture; on the desk, a ceramic baluster lamp by Theodore Deck.*
RIGHT: *Details of the Berber motifs on the paneling; traditional embroidery on a blue background; a painted glass mosque lamp.*

Upon entering the drawing room, the guest senses a striking difference. First of all there is the light: streaming sunlight. Simple lines and sober colors dominate the room, principally the brown and golden stripes of the louver shades and the piercing sunlight, which are reflected in the mirror of a 19th-century Syrian jardinière. The fabrics used to cover the large armchairs are solid colors. The ceiling features traditional motifs of laurel branches. Ecru, green, and earth color are discreet and don't distract from the brilliant play of light. Below the terrace, a date grove stretches out dotted with pink houses.

LEFT: *A Syrian* jardinière *with green Moroccan faience jars.*
OPPOSITE FROM TOP TO BOTTOM: *Details of the shutter inspired by similar ones adorning Turkish houses along the Bosphorus; amber glass teardrops crafted in Egypt; laurel branch marquetry on the ceiling.*
FOLLOWING PAGES: *View of the drawing room and the shutters opening onto the garden.*

Two bedrooms in Tunisia

*Like an aesthete cultivating moments of relaxation during his
Mediterranean sojourns, Alberto Pinto distills a delicate concentrate of
colonial charm in these bedrooms
where a disciple of Henri Matisse once stayed.*

Two Orientalist paintings reminiscent of Matisse set a nonchalant tone within the white walls of the room. An oversized woven-straw screen looms over the bed headboard, draped with a black embroidery from Fez. Several pieces of Portuguese dark wood furniture contribute graphic touches. Guests pass under the rounded curves of a Moorish arch to reach the dressing room and the bath; reflections of mother-of-pearl in the mirrors lighten the latter. Light is the key factor here, opening onto the endless blue of the nearby Mediterranean. The white of the terrace is only interrupted by the black chevrons of the floor tiles.

PAGES 116-117: The straw screen, on which are hung the bold colors of a reclining Moroccan figure by Lucien Fontanarosa and an odalisque by Bezons, is reflected in the large Moroccan silver and wood mirror.
PAGES 118-119: View of the bedroom and bathroom.
ACROSS FROM TOP TO BOTTOM: Detail of a Turkish 18th-century screen of mother-of-pearl and tortoiseshell; a walnut and mother-of-pearl marquetry frame from Syria; wood and ivory inlays on a Spanish commode in the Oriental style.
RIGHT: In the bathroom, a Turkish mirror hangs above the Syrian sink cabinet with mother-of-pearl and bone inlays.
FOLLOWING PAGES: An American leather semainier under a French plaster wall mount from the forties. The harsh sunlight pouring into the room off the terrace is diffused by the sheer cotton and linen embroidered curtains.

A cozier, more feminine suite plays on an attractive harmony of blue, yellow, and white. Filled with Portuguese mahogany furniture, the bedroom is dominated by the elegant canvas of the Russian artist Alexander Rohubtzhof, who resided for many years in Tunisia and worked as a society portraitist of the local bourgeoisie and sojourning Europeans.

The headboard and boxsprings are covered with an antique Persian fabric with Cashmere motifs. The walls of the bathroom are lined with blue, white, and yellow tiles and the inspiration here is a toss up: colonial or Indian, or both?

*LEFT: The Lady in Black by Alexander Rohubtzhof reigns over
Anglo-Indian furnishings.
BELOW: The painted ceiling in the traditional Moroccan style echoes the bed
upholstery in this pale yellow ambience.*

In both these examples, Alberto Pinto proves again his mastery of the design shortcut. Color receives full measure in sharp bold contrasts as does natural light, which seems magnified against the immaculately white limed walls. Furnishings supplement the feel, always fitting into the big picture. Night tables flanking the bed receive souvenirs, and cabinet tops in the bathroom serve as empty canvases for precious silver whatnots and seashells. Refined antique fabrics, delicately embroidered, create intimacy. Nothing escapes Albert Pinto's expert eye as he creates simplicity.

LEFT: The harmony in the bathroom is a cross between traditional Moroccan tiling on the walls and floor and a colonial flavor of lacy white woodwork. OPPOSITE FROM TOP TO BOTTOM: Details of the tiles, the white wooden arch over the bathtub, and an embroidered Persian fabric.

The historical Orient

One approach to Orientalism is a historical one based on the writings
of master architects such as Viollet-le-Duc, whose restorations
called on the forms and colors of the East.
A grouping of painted furniture is the point of departure here.

An Italian desk, chairs, and console in painted wood are the focal points in this room, where Alberto Pinto has concentrated his energy on foregrounding the architectural qualities of the furniture. They are for the experienced eye a perfect case in point of the ornamental vocabulary cherished by Viollet-le-Duc's followers. They are spotlighted like curious trophies: few accessories have been added—a Persian mirror lit by a porcelain lamp from Paris by Jacob Petit and small chests. On the wall over the desk, a quaint painting on leather depicts a stopover in an oasis.

PRECEDING PAGES: A grouping of painted furniture in front of a woven-straw panel; detail of the small Egyptian bookcase.
OPPOSITE FROM TOP TO BOTTOM: Details of the writing desk, a 1900 Persian mirror, and a small mother-of-pearl wedding chest.
RIGHT: Detail of the painted desk.
FOLLOWING PAGES: Under a paneled wood mirror, a mother-of-pearl chest, a bronze teapot, an Indian silver ankle bracelet, and a Jacob Petit lamp.

Calligraphy as design

*The whiteness of the Moroccan architecture that inspired this bedroom
is enticing for its calligraphic decoration composed of downstrokes and upstrokes,
scrolls and arabesques.*

Black and white: the architecture of the bedroom appears to have dictated its decoration in those two colors. The pillars girded at the base by black cement tiles and the plaster stalactites outline the undulating curves of Arabic calligraphy. They trace the limits of three areas, thus affording an impression of space, and separate the dressing area from the bedroom proper. Exalting pure colors, lines and forms, this highly graphic area constitutes a haven of peace. From here and there and spanning different time periods, the pages of calligraphic lettering on the white walls redraft the maps of unknown lands. The black frames emphasize the lines of the Arabic writing, which inspired the Egyptian bedcover, the black-on-beige traditionally crafted tiles in the bathroom, and the lacy wooden wall dividing the bedroom and dressing room. Like a perfect brushstroke, the ecru upholstered headboard with a dark wood frame forms a characteristic Ottoman ogive. The furniture decorated with a fine Anglo-Portuguese marquetry discreetly counterpoints this accomplished exercise in calligraphy.

PAGES 134, 136-137: Views of the bedroom, desk, and the Anglo-Portuguese chaise longue.
PAGE 135: Details of the lacelike wood panels of Indian inspiration in the dressing-room doors.
LEFT: The sophisticated design of the bedroom furnishings attracts the eye, thus attenuating the feeling of height created by the plaster stalactites.
RIGHT, FROM TOP TO BOTTOM: Details of the bedcover; ink calligraphy; the finely crafted traditional tiles covering the bathroom walls.
FOLLOWING PAGES: Art objects and personal souvenirs line an inlaid commode, flanked by a pair of cut-crystal lamps.

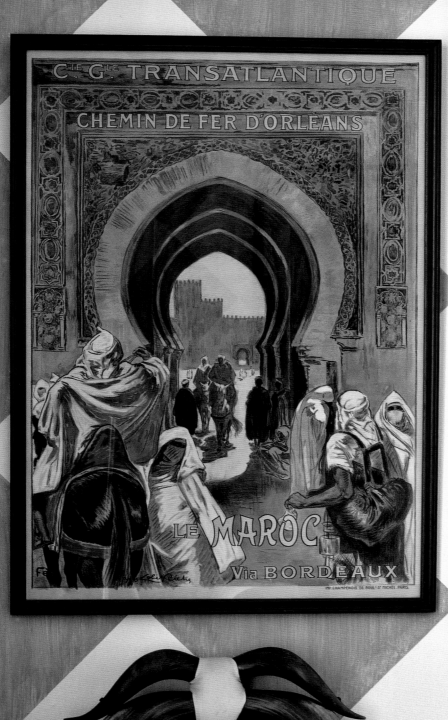

A tribute in green and white to Majorelle

Louis Majorelle, decorator, architect, landscaper and gardener,
was one of the leading figures of Morocco when it was under French rule.
In addition to his blue garden in Marrakech, he left a large oeuvre of imagery
inspired by his journeys to the outskirts of the desert.
This bedroom is a tribute to him.

PLANCHE IV.
HOMME DES HOUCHRA?

PLANCHE II.
FEMME DES CHAAFNA?

PLANCHE III.
FEMME DES AIT-ATTA D'OUREZZA?

PLANCHE I.
FEMME DES AIT-HADIDOU?

A diamond pattern of shades of green on the white wall welcomes the guest. The design alludes to Harlequin, in addition to forming quite an effective visual draw.

The bedroom is in fact dedicated to the days when Morocco was still a French protectorate. Case in point is a travel poster by Majorelle selling the country to tourists. Under it stands a hunting trophy chair concocted from zebu horns.

The adjoining bathroom walls are a more acidulated green in a classic traditional treatment. Zigzag line patterns and painted rosettes on hand-painted tiles contrast with bold diamonds in the bedroom. The silver mirror from India adds unexpected panache.

PAGES 142-143: A 1930s travel poster above an African big-game hunter trophy chair; detail of the diamond wall pattern.

PAGES 144-145: The green-veiled woman in the Majorelle poster above the bed appears to have inspired the tint for the walls. Remarkably stylized, the figure evokes the Western outlook on local folklore and forces a comparison with the framed plates of traditional Moroccan costumes on another wall.

PAGES 146-147: General view of the bedroom.

LEFT: Details of the painted wood sink cabinet with colored glass drawer pulls; juxtaposition of the silver frieze; and star-patterned tiles.

RIGHT: Harmony of green and whites around the delicately painted cabinet.

FOLLOWING PAGES: A silver Indian mirror hangs on traditional Moroccan tiles.

An Ottoman boudoir in Portugal

Through an array of warm contrasts,
the Oriental character of this apartment
has maintained Western reserve.

This Hispano-Moorish drawing room near Lisbon welcomes the white shimmering light off the nearby sea in a bevy of pinks, yellows, and blues. The feel of an apartment has been retained in this relatively limited space. Alberto Pinto has brought the modest dimensions and the sober furnishings into equilibrium by employing original decorative elements, a profusion of forms, exuberant colors, and cross-referencing. The large transparent chandelier bedecked with colored glass flowers comes from Murano, as did those that had hung for centuries in Ottoman residences, whereas 19th-century Europe is represented by low *crapaud* armchairs. The mirror, folding screen, and commode are works of Oriental craftsmen.

PRECEDING PAGES: On a blue lime-washed wall above a bench, a perfectly balanced grouping of 19th-century European porcelain plates and a Turkish mirror, which echo the craftsmanship of the 18th-century folding screen and the mother-of-pearl and tortoiseshell gueridon.

RIGHT: The decorative foliage, flowers, and ribbons of the Murano chandelier in blue and pink accents.

ABOVE: Detail of a yellow and gold porcelain plate on the drawing-room wall.

The sober and simples lines of the settee have almost disappeared under the excessive designs and colors of the antique Moroccan appliqué cover on it. Like three portals closing off a forgotten world, this fabric catches the guest up in whimsical reverie and sets the exotic mood. Each decorative accessory conjures up fragments of a tale spun so long ago that its exact meaning has been forgotten. Perhaps the colorful Spanish porcelain once graced a royal feast, and the white faience parrot lost its motley colors and the gift of speech in one fell swoop. And as for the delicate antique silk cushion embroidered with pastoral designs, it was left behind at the twelfth stroke of midnight.

PRECEDING PAGES: A Turkish mirror in marquetry with a carved pediment is surrounded by decorative plates.
OPPOSITE FROM TOP TO BOTTOM: Details of silk embroidery on a European cushion; a turquoise ceramic turban stand in the shape of a parrot; a pink and gold decorative plate.
RIGHT: View of the boudoir and a sofa covered with a Moroccan appliqué covering.

The pink walls have paled, it would appear, from
centuries of sunlight and the dark haute-époque
Portuguese bed still awaits a long overdue Prince
Charming. The harmony of browns and pinks soft-
ens the mood without it becoming overly sentimental.
The monumental bed steals the show; in fact, it is
the show. A pair of lampshades flanking the bed act
as accents on silent words. These and the other decorative elements are placed against a 19th-century
Portuguese tile dado. This is the artifice that Alberto
Pinto has conjured up to give top billing to an exceptional piece of furniture.

*ABOVE: The pink walls ensure visual continuity between the bedroom and the
bathroom. The sink cabinet and the mirror are in the purest Egyptian style.
RIGHT: The haute-époque Portuguese bed made of turned dark wood stands
majestically in the center of the bedroom.
FOLLOWING PAGES: On the bone-inlaid night table, a still life includes pink
thistles in a Syrian copper and silver vase, an engraved ivory lamp base, and a
plate pinched from the drawing room.*

The white immaculate bedroom has made the crossing from Gibraltar and is now in Morocco, in this light-drenched place filled with allusions to North Africa. The Gio Ponti copper bed has as its four posts stylized warrior lances that have been neutralized by four perfect spheres. The headboard is a wide band of stamped copper decorated with a row of five Turkish bouquets of lobed rosettes.

Two small lamps in repoussé copper have been placed on a bone-inlaid Syrian secretaire. An armchair with a leather seat and back would be fitting for a tribal chief.

ABOVE: The copper bed with repoussé and stamped designs by Gio Ponti.
RIGHT: Two silver lamps rest on a marquetry secretaire under three antique
Moroccan ceramic plates. In the background hangs an Indian mirror against
antique hand-painted Moroccan tiles.

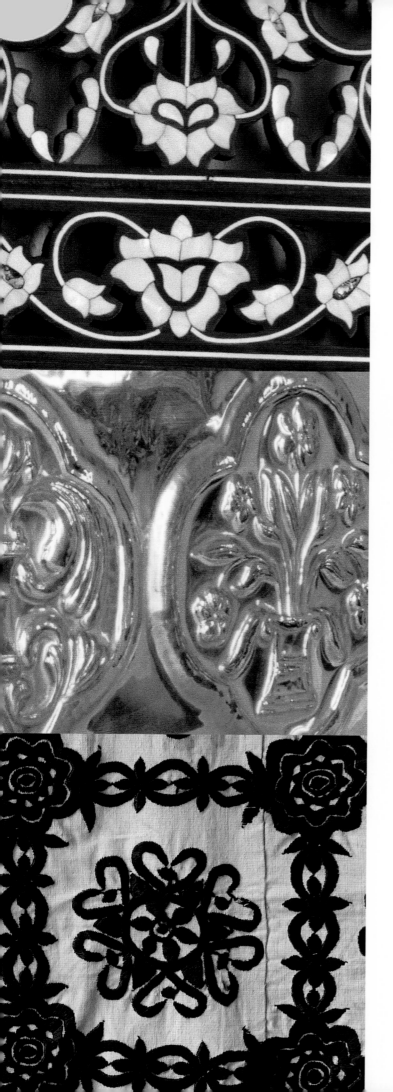

Here and there on the walls hang antique Moroccan ceramic plates in yellow, green, and blue, the same colors as the tiles with traditional star and rosette motifs in the bathroom. The accessories are in keeping with the North African theme and complete the sober Orientalist composition: copper candlesticks with calligraphic designs and silver boxes, a large mirror surrounded by delicate mother-of-pearl inlaid scrolls facing the repoussé metal frame of the bathroom mirror, Syrian furniture, and Oriental paintings.

LEFT: Details of the marquetry of the Syrian mirror, the copper band of the bed headboard, and an antique Moroccan embroidery.
RIGHT: The mirror and the copper candlesticks come from Syria as does the wooden marquetry commode.

A drawing room in Tangiers

The Western eye is attracted by highly elaborate interiors within essentially
white structures: an apt description of Moroccan palaces.
Here Alberto Pinto has created a rare osmosis between Oriental tradition
and European fantasies.

Visible in the distance as soon as the guest enters the residence, the formal drawing room plays on marked contrasts to glorify its exceptional architecture.

The white walls appear to surge from the floor, spangled with the reds and greens of rugs. Generous sunlight outlines the most minute detail of the ornate plasterwork on the arches, moldings, and friezes around the room.

PRECEDING PAGES: Across from an Orientalist canvas by Antonio Manuel da Fonseca (1796-1890) hangs an opaline and Bohemian crystal chandelier. Velvet capitonné silver armchairs from India cohabit with a Hispano-Moorish commode in macassar wood and ivory.
Indian miniatures are grouped around a mirror, under the stern eye of an Algerian tribal chief in terracotta by Joseph Le Gluch.
LEFT: Italian silver vases occupy the mantelpiece of an English faience fireplace in the Chinese style, above a painting of children by Alexis Courajod.
ABOVE: On a walnut and mother-of-pearl gueridon sits a vase full of tiny silver and straw fans.

In this interior the decorator exercised no control over his passion for collecting. Silver objets d'art, Indian miniatures, vases, and lamps are arranged on gueridons and end tables and attest to his abiding love for the rare and the unusual.

LEFT: *Chinese-style English mantelpiece, Indian armchair, and a 19th-century Turkish gueridon.*
ABOVE: *A ceramic lamp by Dorothy Thorpe stands near painted glass mosque lamps used as cachepots.*
The wooden throne behind is from Zanzibar.

The luminosity is largely due to the glut of white covering all the architectural surfaces but also comes from the crisp chromatic harmonies assembled by Pinto.

A whole palette of greens from acidulated to refined, soft tones bring to mind England's top interior designers from the 1960s. To heat up this cool chromatic scale, the violet velvet covering the armchairs adds zesty pep.

PRECEDING PAGES: View of the windows flanked with Indian portraits painted on glass. A Mogul offering coffer stands in perfect alignment with the arches.
LEFT: Details of green and white embroidery covering the sofas and a 19th-century Anglo-Indian gaming table in pewter and ivory.
RIGHT: Reflected in a Turkish mirror, a ceramic parrot swings on a perch above three Mogul ewers.

A vacation house in Tangiers

*Alberto Pinto has imagined a timeless update for this traditional home,
based on comfort, luxury, and his own very personal concept of
design geography, which situates Morocco, India, China, and Turkey
within a common territory.*

The garden constitutes an integral part of Oriental domestic architecture. Guests enter the house and then walk along a vestibule, which is actually a peristyle opening onto nature. With its numerous potted plants, this space serves as an antechamber to the garden, separated from the living area by Andalusian grilles. The ambiguity between interior and exterior—a confusion dear to the Hispano-Moorish architectural tradition—is maintained by the brick floor, whitewashed walls, and nomadic furnishings, principally illuminated by candlelight and wrought-iron lanterns.

PAGE 180: The entrance: above a French marble table from the 1940s hangs a carved and painted Moroccan wooden mirror. PAGE 181: View of the gallery; the patterned brick floor is covered by a sisal runner.
ABOVE: A collection of silver hands of Fatima are presented on a wall of the entranceway.
RIGHT: Indian portraits frame an ogive arched window opening onto the garden.
PAGE 184: Details of the French windows. PAGE 185: The golden brown Hispano-Moorish plates date from the late 16th century.

Ignoring the clichés associating China with gold and the eponymous red, Alberto Pinto saw the Chinese drawing room in white—the Western symbol of purity as well as the traditional choice for walls in North African houses because of its reflective capacities. Here the color enhances the furniture and a collection of Asian works of art. On an immaculate, wide divan, large cushions serve as dividers. They are covered in blue and mauve Chinese fabrics using the same traditional motifs that embellish the closionné enamel console on which a Burmese wooden Buddha sits. The vast horseshoe arch bay windows with interlacing wood decoration are the most obvious cues to Orientalism.

PAGE 186: General view of the white drawing room. PAGE 187: A Burmese Buddha seems to levitate above a Chinese cloisonné enameled table.
LEFT: An Italian wrought-iron and metal chandelier hangs above immaculately white European furnishings.
ABOVE: View of the dining room from the Chinese drawing room.
FOLLOWING PAGES: A red lacquered Chinese screen is the backdrop for a collection of Indian silver boxes.

Communicating with the Chinese drawing room by a large horseshoe arch, the dining room welcomes a flock of parrots alighted on deep green papyrus stems running down the center of the table. The pink and yellow table settings are snazzy and spring-like, awash in daylight entering through four bay windows that are identical to those of the drawing room. Two great 18th-century Chinese blue and white porcelain pots extend the Far Eastern theme of the adjacent room. The room has large windows overlooking the sea, natural wood furniture, and large mirrors, and the natural light and the land-scape are both essential features of the design.

LEFT: An 18th-century painting of the French school, Urn with Parrots *looms over a bone-inlaid Persian commode and announces to guests the bird theme awaiting them on the dining table.*
Chairs from the 1930s by the American designer Frances Elkin surround the table with feathery papyrus fronds bending down.

As Pinto has imagined it, the dining room can be transformed on a whim. On a light-hearted day, a forest of papyrus envelops the cheery table. On a more decorous occasion, the Chinese blue and white features can play a leading role. Pink table linens turn the mood to the 1940s and particularly enhance the Chinese porcelain vases and consoles. The decorator need only follow his fancy and dress a colorful table like a still life to please and captivate guests.

LEFT: Two monumental 18th-century blue and white Chinese porcelain vases flank a Moroccan-style bay window.
A gilt wrought-iron ceiling light hangs nearby.
ABOVE: A voluptuous sculpted wood sea nymph from the Louis XV period leans on a console in front of a Venetian mirror.
FOLLOWING PAGES: The sea nymph rules over a bright blue and pink table with a marine theme.

Arabian Nights

*Bright colors are disapproved of here in the realm of
nuance and refinement.
The tumultuous romanticism of Delacroix has been abandoned in favor of
the shadowy, dreamlike interpretation of
the poète maudit, Gérard de Nerval.*

In this bewitching dining room, luncheons take place within silvered walls illuminated by natural daylight; in the evening a softened lavender blue ambience accompanies dinners with the arabesque wall designs in the flickering candlelight. The space takes on a different atmosphere depending on the time of day or night. Traditional cues have been blurred consciously. The silvery arabesques have been enlarged and repeated on the wall, losing their Oriental register and becoming more medieval in character. But when night falls, the lights of the chandelier twinkle, the marquetry surfaces of the furniture shine, and candles glow: the perfect moment for Scheherazade to step forward wrapped in diaphanous veils.

PRECEDING PAGES: Facing the door, a fireplace encased in Venetian mirrors is surmounted by a Turkish mirror. Opaline and crystal wall lamps are reminders of the Ottoman taste for Bohemian glass.
LEFT: The imposing porcelain and crystal chandelier calls to mind the Turkish palaces on the Bosphorus, and the wall lights in the Baccarat style render a soft, gossamer brilliance, which is reflected, repeated, and obscured by the lacy plasterwork covering the ceiling and the vast mirror hidden behind it.
FOLLOWING PAGES: Crystal glasses and candlesticks and blue opaline vases stand on Syrian consoles, and the play of light and transparency is repeated ad infinitum *like an endless enfilade of rooms in a storybook palace.*

The European romantic style is interpreted here *à l'orientale* through the furniture and the Charles X decorations in blackened pear wood and mother-of-pearl. This transformation could be pursued further: the silvered painted arabesques metamorphose into precious wooden chair backs or into white embroidery on the blue velvet upholstery. The dining table is supported by an elegant and massive leg assembly of mother-of-pearl, ivory, and wood marquetry: a masterpiece of craftsmanship. Four banded spheres, like globes of unknown worlds, emerge from under the shadows of the tabletop.

LEFT: Detail of the leg assembly of the dining table in mother-of-pearl, bone, and ebony marquetry, after a design by Alberto Pinto.
ABOVE: A chair back in a marquetry using the same materials as the table.

The Orient in Paris

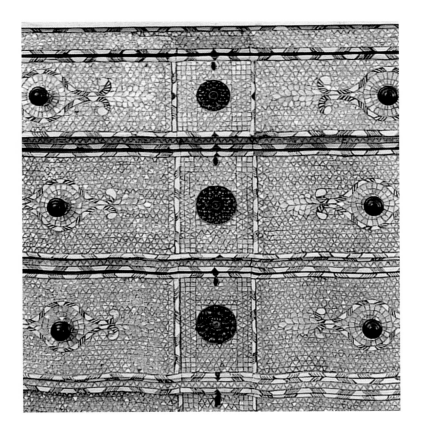

Over the years the enlightened Orient has often guided Alberto Pinto when he prepared tables for festive occasions. Here is a case in point in the apartment that the author Paul Morand once occupied.
Caned Regency chairs stand around a dressed table, majestic Syrian armchairs line the walls, mother-of-pearl mirrors hang on 18th-century wood paneling. This Parisian dining room reflects the perfect marriage of classicism and Orientalism

The stripped wood paneling acts as a perfect foil for the Moroccan ceramic plates hanging on it, the *point de Hongrie* oak parquet floor, and the designs on the Moroccan rug. Although the original spirit of the room has been conserved, thanks to a shrewd selection of furnishings an Oriental feeling has taken over here in the center of Paris.

Against walls of mirrors, an imposing Syrian armoire with its inlaid arabesques stands in state, as if suspended in space surrounded by infinite reflections. Sensory perceptions are confused, dimensions blurred, and the Orient materializes as in a mirage.

PRECEDING PAGES: Views of the dining room and a detail of the marquetry commode. Two tables have been set, each creating its own mood.
ABOVE: Lavishly embellished with mother of pearl,
a Syrian commode supports a stoup overflowing with irises.
RIGHT: French classicism and the Orient are brought face to face in evening candlelight.

The romantic East

*Excessive and frivolous, this boudoir given over to feminine confabs is awash
with tender colors, light materials, and delicate forms.*

Quintessentially feminine, the small drawing room is designed like a boudoir in shades of green and parma where women can chat and discuss far from men. Frills is the word here: tiny pompoms dance on the bottom of the lampshades and green feathers edge the cushions on the deep floral-print sofas. The vases and other accessories are delicate and precious in ivory, mother of pearl, repoussé copper, glass, and opaline. The Indian furniture seems the perfect answer to a grown-up little girl's once-upon-a-time dreams where she imagines herself a princess, or why not empress?

PAGES 222-223: *View of the boudoir where an Egyptian commode and Indian silver armchairs and tables cohabit; detail of the silver armchair.*
PAGES 224-225: *The sofa is flanked by Murano glass lamps from the 1940s; above hang a series of plates of traditional Moroccan costumes by Besancenot.*
LEFT: *Details of three traditional Moroccan embroideries from Rabat and Fez.*
RIGHT: *An Indian silver armchair stands by an Egyptian commode with bone inlays.*

Abandoning the Parma violet, but staying true to the green, Alberto Pinto creates an ambiguous ambience in the adjoining bath while conserving the excess of the boudoir. Traditional Moroccan ceramic tiles cover the wall behind the bathtub and, in combination with marble slabs, the floor. Fine, light blown-glass perfume flacons with gilt highlights add airiness. Like plaster lace, the self-indulgent, deeply irregular fluting arches above the tub. The audacious craftsmanship was well worth it: the contrasting materials, the white volutes against the water-green background, reflected in the large mirror above the sink cabinet, create elegant flamboyance and flair.

LEFT: On a Syrian gueridon, a blown glass vase harmonizes with the colors of the tiled floor and walls.
RIGHT FROM TOP TO BOTTOM: Enameled Moroccan ceramics; detail of a contemporary Morrocan rug; ceramic tiles.

LEFT: Built into a tiled alcove, the bathtub with a marble border is the place for tranquil moments of relaxation.
ABOVE: The sink cabinet is installed in a mosaic-lined niche decorated with ancient motifs.
FOLLOWING PAGES: A bouquet of anemones and tall perfume flacons of blown glass stand next to a large mirror.

A bedroom in the Sahara

*Facing the ever-renewing blue of the Mediterranean, two bedrooms were quite
naturally outfitted in the color of the sky.*

Tuareg blue sets the theme in the bedroom with a direct reference to the men in blue from the desert. During the several nights that a guest will spend here surrounded by black, blue, and white, set off by a plaster frieze like an embroidered band encircling the interior of a tent, he is invited to become one with the fantasies of nomadic lifestyle. The choice is unambiguously manifest: a series of engravings of traditional Moroccan costumes in the style of Majorelle line a wall, and the furniture is based on early 20th-century models reminiscent of Bugatti crafted in the Orient. The deep Tuareg blue presented in bands transforms its spirit into one of seaside gaiety while idealizing the desert tribes.

PRECEDING PAGES: Echoing a charmingly simple style of life, the objects in the bedroom appear to have been chosen for their unrefined beauty: lamp bases and vases in blown blue glass, a hammered metal teapot, the roughly finished bronze floor lamps by Antonioz like desert warrior lances, and a small decorative wall cabinet and matching desk with Syrian marquetry after Bugatti.
On the wall hang plates of traditional costumes by Besancenot.
RIGHT: Black and white are discreetly present in the decorative plates hanging on the walls and the fabric covering the sofa.
FOLLOWING PAGES: The armoire and flanking armchairs crafted using Middle Eastern techniques, images of traditional costumes, and the bronze floor lamp musingly evoke a 1920s pipedream Orient.

Two blue bedrooms

*Facing the ever-renewing blue of the Mediterranean,
two bedrooms were quite naturally outfitted in the color of the sky.*

White walls and floor accented by unadulterated deep blue highlights of the moldings and archways: the game plan here is to play pure color. A similar strategy was used in choosing furnishings that are sober and practical. Color structures the space. A theatrical arch separates the bedroom from the bath, where a mother-of-pearl inlaid mirror hangs. Caribbean-style latticework and ceramic tiles in blue and white pass the light around the room, making it hum gaily.

PRECEDING PAGES: Two wide armchairs flanking the bed are from Central Europe; the blue bedcover with white interlacing patterns is from Egypt. Above the bed, the bath is visible through an interior window.
LEFT: View of the blue and white bathroom of wood, marble, and ceramic tiles.
RIGHT FROM TOP TO BOTTOM: Details of the Egyptian bedcover, latticework, and a traditional fabric.

A fascination with the seascape that offers a wide view of the bay led to the luminous blue chosen to for this bedroom. Bringing into play the traditional colors of Mediterranean houses, blue and white, it has the immediate effect of transporting guests to sunny beaches near the waters linking Spain and Morocco. Traditional Berber pottery, with its rustic roughness and simple designs, enhances the North African references and opens the portal to faraway lands.

OPPOSITE AND ABOVE: Antique Berber pots seem to come straight from an archaeological dig. A collection of photos from the 1950s on the walls turns the clock back to a nostalgic past.
FOLLOWING PAGES: The blue walls of the bedroom opening onto the sea blend with that of the Mediterranean.

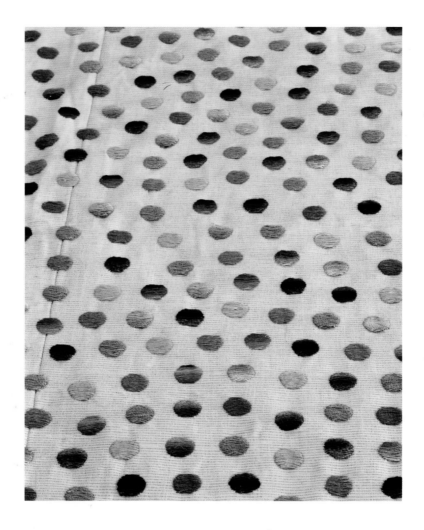

ABOVE: Detail of the cotton embroidered bedcovers.
RIGHT: Hung askance, as is the matching one over the bed,
the mirror sets the bath spinning.